GOOD

Georgette Butcher [...]
years Manager of [...]
the Scripture Un[...]
formal retirement [...] became
Editor of the influential magazine, *The Chris-*
tian Bookseller.

She is the author of *Moments With God*, also
published by Fount.

By the same author, available
from Fount Paperbacks

MOMENTS WITH GOD

GOODNIGHT, LORD

Georgette Butcher

Collins
FOUNT PAPERBACKS

First published in Great Britain by
Fount Paperbacks, London in 1988

Copyright © Georgette Butcher 1988

Printed and bound in Great Britain by
William Collins Sons & Co. Ltd, Glasgow

CONDITIONS OF SALE

This book is sold subject to the condition
that it shall not, by way of trade or otherwise,
be lent, re-sold, hired out or otherwise circulated
without the publisher's prior consent in any form of
binding or cover other than that in which it is
published and without a similar condition
including this condition being imposed
on the subsequent purchaser

BIBLE REFERENCES

All Bible References are taken from the Good News
Bible and are used by permission of Collins Publish-
ers and the Bible Society.
Old Testament copyright © American Bible Society,
New York 1976; New Testament copyright ©
American Bible Society, New York 1966, 1971, and
4th edition 1976

1

In the beginning, when God created the universe, the earth was formless and desolate. The raging ocean that covered everything was engulfed in total darkness, and the power of God was moving over the water. Then God commanded, "Let there be light" – and light appeared. God was pleased with what he saw. Then he separated the light from the darkness, and he named the light "Day" and the darkness "Night". Evening passed and morning came – that was the first day.

Genesis 1:1–5

Whatever we may think about how the world began one thing we cannot deny; there is day and there is night.

Have you ever thought about the way in which we, as civilized folk, manage our day? – all the business of dressing, undressing, bathing, cleaning our teeth. Going to work or coping with a home and children, day after day, doing more or less the same things. Routines, habits, all are a part of being a human being.

At the end of the day after the work which has taken up our time, we wind down, relax and eventually reach our bed. If we thank God for what we term our blessings, I imagine that we thank him then for the warmth and comfort of preparing for sleep.

Our bodies and minds need the time of rest that night gives to us, and as we prepare for oblivion our thoughts may well travel over the day. How has it been? Good and satisfying?

Sometimes the end of the day does leave us with a sense of discomfort, and it is always a good thing to go back to find out where it comes from. It could be something that was repeated that perhaps should not have been passed on, or a less than kind word spoken about another person. Perhaps it was something to do with work, or with family or children. Whatever it is I find it needs to be pulled out, as it were, and faced. Often it is not a question of asking forgiveness from anyone – this may not be possible – but a steady determination that in future we will accept God's help as we cope with the day. Sometimes asking God that words spoken can be forgotten will help. Whatever it may be – omission or commission – to face and speak about it with God at the end of the day does settle the mind – and the stomach – wonderfully.

God made the day and we do all the things that have to be done, things that as Christians we believe are what he has given to us to do. He also made the night when we rest and recuperate. He is the Creator, and not only did he create the world but he also made us, every wonderful working part. Tomorrow is another day, and if today is settled and finished with it could be a good one.

✳

I praise you because you are the Creator and upholder of all things, and for the wonders and workings of the body you have given me. Make me a whole person, sensitive to the Spirit and glorifying you in all my days.

Goodnight, Lord

2

Give thanks to the LORD,
   proclaim his greatness;
   tell the nations what he
   has done.
Sing praise to the LORD;
   Tell of the wonderful things
   he has done.
Be glad that we belong to him;
   let all who worship him rejoice.
Go to the Lord for help;
   And worship him continually.

                    Psalm 105: 1–4

How is it that God manages to convey his message to his children through even the most ordinary means and in ways that we ourselves would never think about? When *Beyond Healing*, a book by Jennifer Rees Larcombe, was published I was asked if I would interview her. This lady – the daughter of Tom Rees, a well-known evangelist of his day, and Jean, his equally well-known wife – had contracted an incurable disease, and in the years of adjustment wrote a book about the experience and the question of healing as it affected her. The interview had to be over the phone, and in the minutes before the due time, whilst putting together some questions, I imagined her in her wheelchair, and even wondered whether she were able to hold the phone.

The moment came, I dialled, and immediately a firm confident *loving* voice answered. We spoke together for some fifteen minutes, and at the end I was constrained to say that she had not sounded at all as I had expected. She asked me how she had sounded, and after telling her she said that she was pleased, because that was what she had been praying for.

What had God done in that experience? In my case he had made me aware of his love. Through Jennifer Larcombe's voice I had heard his love, and it had come over as love for me. This feeling was with me in all its strength for several days, and the memory is still there. Perhaps through my words Jennifer herself had perceived that God was answering her prayer, and that she too was especially receiving his love.

Day after day God uses us to convey something of his love and caring to others. The more open we are to him, the more he can use us. It is not always words; it is often actions or attitudes that most convey a message. Perhaps today has not seemed to be a great day for either giving or receiving. But if we let him, God works through us, and we may not be at all conscious of him doing so. Similarly we do not always know when God is doing his work within us. It may just be happening through the circumstances of a normal day.

So a prayer each morning to be available and open, both to give and to receive, may mean real blessing.

***

Father, I do long to show something of you to others. I want to be so close to you in my thoughts that inevitably you are seen.

Goodnight, Lord

3

Do not judge others, so that God will not judge you, for God will judge you in the same way as you judge others, and he will apply to you the same rules you apply to others. Why, then, do you look at the speck in your brother's eye, and pay no attention to the log in your own eye? How dare you say to your brother, "Please let me take that speck out of your eye", when you have a log in your own eye? You hypocrite! First take the log out of your own eye, and then you will be able to see clearly to take the speck out of your brother's eye.   Matthew 7:1–5

However few people we meet in a day, it is often impossible to get through it without having received in one way or another some action or word that hurts. It could happen in a shop or supermarket, in the office or at the school gate amongst the mothers waiting for their children. It could be a driver who cuts in or turns after a late signal.

Perhaps it is just a small thing, an unresponsive attitude, a laugh or joke that appears to cut us out. Not really terribly important – any of it – but it makes us hurt.

Instead of concentrating on the other person and wondering why they acted as they did, perhaps we should wonder about our own reaction. Thinking it through often helps us to understand why we reacted so violently. The unfortunate thing is that until we ourselves feel aggrieved it is very easy to forget the kind of effect that we may be having on others. We can so easily hurt others by our attitudes; it is likely to be without wanting to do so, just as they would not want to hurt us.

So we are back to love and how love manifests itself, not only in the way in which we treat one another but also in the way in which we react to each other. Two sentences from Amy Carmichael's book *If* sum it up very well: "If a sudden jar can cause me to speak an impatient, unloving word, then I know nothing of Calvary love", and "If I do not give a friend the 'benefit of the doubt' but put the worst construction instead of the best on what is said or done, then I know nothing of Calvary love."

Has today been one in which it appears that an arrow has been flung straight at you? Thinking about it can make the wound fester. In other words, we become hard and resentful inside. This is where we need the other dimension of forgiving and forgetting, not allowing the hurt to rankle, but divesting ourselves of it as quickly as possible and allowing our Lord's love to fill us afresh.

✳✳✳

Dear Lord, I give to you all the things that have happened today that caused me to react in an unloving way. The hurt that I may have given and those things that hurt me. I ask your forgiveness and pray that they may be put aside and forgotten.

Goodnight, Lord

4

Let us give thanks to the God and Father of our Lord Jesus Christ, the merciful Father, the God from whom all help comes! He helps us in all our troubles, so that we are able to help others who have all kinds of troubles, using the same help that we ourselves have received from God. Just as we have a share in Christ's many sufferings, so also through Christ we share in God's great help. If we suffer, it is for your help and salvation; if we are helped, then you too are helped and given the strength to endure with patience the same sufferings that we also endure. So our hope in you is never shaken; we know that just as you share in our sufferings, you also share in the help we receive.   2 Corinthians 1:3–7

In a book written by Gordon Thomas concerning celibacy in the Roman Catholic Church, one of his characters, a priest, is standing by the death bed of a woman. The woman's husband turns to him and says that the priest should be glad he will never feel the pain of losing a loved wife.

As I read these words, others came immediately into my mind, "There are other pains!"

Today we have mixed with and met many people, some of whom we know quite well perhaps, but others who are mere acquaintances, and some entire strangers. We know the circumstances of our friends and those close to us in the family; the outward situations that affect each one. There are the times when we see that those situations bring hurt, sorrow and disillusionment, and we can offer strength and encouragement. But the inner pains, those that are not so obvious, these are hidden pains.

Sometimes the pain that you are bearing today may seem the worst in the whole world, but there are other pains, and any one of those people you met today may also be bearing one.

We must never allow ourselves to feel that everything goes wrong just for us alone. Life on earth is never made up of always being at peace and walking in the sunshine. Every Christian's life is made up of disappointments, unfulfilled longings, partings with loved ones, sickness and all the other things that can come to shatter us.

As the priest listened to the words of the bereaved husband he could perhaps have said, "Not for you the pain of never having the love of a wife, or the joy of children". We may never gauge another's anguish, and although we may often think of those we meet as being without suffering, we cannot know whether the pain of not having children could be just as great for one person as the loss of a child for another. The more obvious heartbreaks can be seen, but we need to remember as we meet and mingle with people that there are other pains, pains which are often completely hidden.

❋

Keep me sensitive to the needs and pains of others. Help me to support and understand the burdens of my fellow beings.

Goodnight, Lord

5

Do not use harmful words, but only helpful words, the kind that build up and provide what is needed, so that what you say will do good to those who hear you. And do not make God's Holy Spirit sad; for the Spirit is God's mark of ownership on you, a guarantee that the Day will come when God will set you free. Get rid of all bitterness, passion, and anger. No more shouting or insults, no more hateful feelings of any sort. Instead, be kind and tender-hearted to one another, and forgive one another, as God has forgiven you through Christ.

Ephesians 4:29–32

Have you noticed that when we espouse a cause it is still possible for us as Christians to believe that we are right and everyone else is wrong? And not only causes, but denominations, beliefs, politics, even a simple way of doing something can cause schisms and splits between groups, churches and families.

Love often flies out of the window when two people cannot agree. It also seems to turn into active hatred when some major issue is at stake. When we look around the world we see trouble, distress, famine and wars, people not only failing to understand one another, but not even wanting to try to understand. That is perhaps the saddest thing: to be so deeply entrenched in our own position that there is not even the thought of trying to see the issue from the other person's point of view.

What makes us so sure we are right in the way we think? Could there possibly be another side to the whole issue, that we refuse to see?

Some people are able to see both sides of a question, which can make it difficult when a decision has to be made! Undoubtedly there will be issues when a stand does have to be taken, but do we then "shout"? Are our words hurtful? A loving, gentle attitude can bring peace into a situation, and what God wants is far more important than the way in which we want things to be done. It may not be so simple to change things and attitudes out in the wider world, but it is certainly possible to examine the way we think about them, and we can refuse to condemn in hate those who think or do things differently.

It is also possible to make sure that an entrenched attitude within our home, work or church circle is not causing distress to others.

✻✻✻

Help me, Father, to see things from your point of view, and to understand more the ways in which I should react and act in every situation that arises.

Goodnight, Lord

6

I have told you this so that my joy may be in you
and that your joy may be complete. My commandment is this: love one another, just as I love you.
The greatest love a person can have for his friends
is to give his life for them. And you are my friends
if you do what I command you. I do not call you
servants any longer, because a servant does not
know what his master is doing. Instead, I call you
friends, because I have told you everything I have
heard from my Father.   John 15:11–15

"I'm doing this for *your* friends!" Something had gone
wrong as I was preparing for the visit of the home
group, and I just spoke those words to the Lord. I was
resentful; I had the feeling that as the effort I was
making was for fellow Christians nothing should have
gone wrong. Was there also a feeling that they were not
entirely *my* friends? Whatever was the deep-rooted
reason behind those words, two of them — "your
friends" — have stayed with me.

There are still places in the world where hospitality
means sharing, or even giving, the last of food or drink
to the stranger who enters the home. Hospitality in the
West is much more formal and less automatic. Friendship can usually claim it, and we also have a special
feeling for the friends of friends and an obligation to
help such people. We feel quickly at ease with them
because of the link that we both have with the mutual

friend. How often people say, "A friend of A — 's is a friend of mine".

Are we really conscious, though, that people whom we meet are the friends of Jesus? Because in some strange way friendship seems to be a much more personal thing than even saying that we belong to the family of God. As Christians we do belong to this family, of course, but the thought of friendship brings out a more intimate aspect.

Friends are special, chosen, very much a part of one's life. There is a different relationship with each one, very much in the way that Jesus deals with each of us in a different way. When he asks us or expects us to give to his friends it is the mutual friendship that binds us together.

I find now that thinking of Christians whom I come into contact with as personal friends of Jesus is quite awe-inspiring. And sometimes it is very much as if he is standing there watching the way that I am treating them. What I do for and how I behave towards the friends of Jesus I realize I should do because they are the friends of a Friend. My love, respect and honour for him is extended to them. It is worth keeping that thought in mind.

✳✳✳

Your friendship is precious and real to me, Lord. Help me to remember that you have other friends, and to extend to them the love, help and hospitality that you expect from those who have a mutual friendship with you.

Goodnight, Lord

7

Praise God in his Temple!
  Praise his strength in heaven!
Praise him for the mighty things
  he has done.
  Praise his supreme greatness.
Praise him with trumpets.
  Praise him with harps and lyres.
Praise him with drums and dancing.
  Praise him with harps and flutes.
Praise him with cymbals.
  Praise him with loud cymbals.
Paise the LORD, all living creatures!
Praise the LORD!

Psalm 150

A book containing a collection of writings came into my hands, and as I looked through it I was struck by the fact that in all its four hundred pages only eight were devoted to praise. Admittedly the book was in sections and was meant to cover the stages in a Christian walk. Nevertheless the quota for words of praise seemed woefully small.

It made me wonder how much time God's children devote to praising him, whether in fellowship or in private, and what exactly we mean by praise. Our psalm tonight could well convince us that praise is equated with noise, but it is not so much that musical instruments are noisy as the fact that we are using them to show praise. A singer uses his or her voice to praise God; it is not necessarily the result but the act that praises.

Praise can be the acknowledgement in the heart that God *is*. It can be the deep sigh of contentment as one looks out at beauty and realizes that it all comes from the Creator.

But as love can be expressed in actions, yet sometimes needs to be said in words, so praise for and to our God needs to be vocalized.

The deliberate quietening of the heart and mind, the refusal to allow the burdens and problems to be poured out, the putting of God first in our time with him, rather than our needs, is the lead in to praise. For a little time we allow our mind to contain thoughts purely of him, to think of him as the Almighty, the great one, upholding all things. We remember that he has touched us, wanted us, and as we marvel it seems that we can know the beauty of his presence, and our heart responds to him.

✳✳✳

I lift up my heart, my hands and my voice in praise to you, my God. May the worship of my being please you.

Goodnight, Lord

8

All of us were like sheep that were lost, each of us going his own way. But the LORD made the punishment fall on him, the punishment all of us deserved. He was treated harshly, but endured it humbly; he never said a word. Like a lamb about to be slaughtered, like a sheep about to be sheared, he never said a word. He was arrested and sentenced and led off to die, and no one cared about his fate. He was put to death for the sins of our people. He was placed in a grave with evil men, he was buried with the rich, even though he had never committed a crime or ever told a lie.

The LORD says, "It was my will that he should suffer, his death was a sacrifice to bring foregiveness. And so he will see his descendants; he will live a long life, and through him my purpose will succeed."   Isaiah 53:6–10

How would you feel if you were told that, although everyone knew that you were perfectly innocent, you had been chosen to bear the punishment of a group of miscreants?

Many a child, loudly proclaiming innocence, has been hauled home by a parent after some sort of group childish prank, and just "being on the spot" has been enough to proclaim guilt, at least in the eyes of a mother or father.

There have been hostages who have been taken and killed, innocent yet dying for a reason they cannot comprehend. If we think of these examples, dimly we begin to see the tremendous sacrifice that Jesus made when, completely free from any cause for the punishment, he had to die. The picture that the words of Isaiah makes for us is stark and vivid. *We* have gone astray – the punishment was laid on him.

How would each of us feel if we were in a situation where someone saved us from death but in doing so died himself? I am fairly certain that we would feel remorse and guilt. We would endeavour in some way to make up for the death we did not die, but should have done.

Why did God allow his Son to die in a plan conceived and executed over such a space of time? He did it because of his great love for us.

Perhaps we need to ponder afresh on just what that love and that death actually means to us tonight. And just how we are living our lives because of it.

***

Through death comes life. Thank you for the death that gives me eternal life. Help me to live my life in the light of Jesus's death and your gift of heaven

Goodnight, Lord

9

Every year the parents of Jesus went to Jerusalem for the Passover Festival. When Jesus was twelve years old, they went to the festival as usual. When the festival was over, they started back home, but the boy Jesus stayed in Jerusalem. His parents did not know this; they thought that he was with the group, so they travelled a whole day and then started looking for him among their relatives and friends. They did not find him, so they went back to Jerusalem looking for him. On the third day they found him in the Temple, sitting with the Jewish teachers, listening to them and asking questions. All who heard him were amazed at his intelligent answers. His parents were astonished when they saw him, and his mother said to him, "My son, why have you done this to us? Your father and I have been terribly worried trying to find you."

He answered them, "Why did you have to look for me? Didn't you know that I had to be in my Father's house?" But they did not understand his answer.   Luke 2:41–49

Mary and Joseph had faced a traumatic experience when they were betrothed and realized that there was to be a child. Together and separately it had been something that had to be faced in the context of family and village life.

They had had tremendous experiences – visions from

God and the knowledge that what was happening was being allowed by him. Eventually, after Jesus was born the days settled and life became that of any normal family who had to work and do the myriad things that keep a home going.

We have no way of knowing whether their son Jesus was any different from other children. One can assume that he ran and played and did what the other boys did. But certainly they would not forget this day when he was twelve years old and they lost him. It was the sort of thing that parents dread – everything seemingly normal and under control, and then from one moment to the next disaster falls.

The period from the first moment of wondering what could have happened to the time when knowledge comes can seem very long indeed. Mary and Joseph searched for three days. The outcome was a happy one, although they failed to understand what Jesus was trying to explain to them about the episode.

Every day something happens to someone that brings grief and perhaps guilt. One day it could well happen to you or to me. The days of uncertainty that have to be gone through, the results of medical tests that have to be faced, the knock on the door in the middle of the night, or the ring of the telephone – we don't look for these things or expect them but we are wise if day after day we allow God to teach us of himself. Then our life is truly one of abiding and, when difficult times come, we are able to draw on his strength.

❋

Keep me faithful day by day, Father, getting to know you more. May our relationship be strengthened into a firm knowledge of you as my God.

Goodnight, Lord

10

Israel, why then do you complain that the LORD doesn't know your troubles or care if you suffer injustice? Don't you know? Haven't you heard? The LORD is the everlasting God; he created all the world. He never grows tired or weary. No one understands his thoughts. He strengthens those who are weak and tired. Even those who are young grow weak; young men can fall exhausted. But those who trust in the LORD for help will find their strength renewed. They will rise on wings like eagles; they will run and not get weary, they will walk and not grow weak.   Isaiah 40:27–31

The last sentence in *The Power Factor*, a book by George and Meg Paterson, reads "The Power Factor ultimately is total obedience to the words of God. You find it when you seek for it with all your heart."

I believe that there are many among us who are spiritually hungry, suffering from malnutrition of the soul. They are people who day after day go through all the mundane tasks and routines, faithfully undertake spiritual exercises, are kind and loving to friends, family and strangers, and yet at rock bottom have a deep dissatisfaction. It may not be something that is always apparent, but sometimes in moments of quiet or in the dark hours of the night there is a feeling of emptiness.

At that moment, if we are honest, we understand that the answer is – God. That moment of honesty strips away all the good deeds, the "trying", church attendance, even counselling, and we realize that although much is good there is still something missing.

In *The Power Factor* we read "You can remain a hen, or a grounded eagle in a hen run, forever tormented by a vague conviction that life should somehow be different from what it is. Or you can be an eagle liberated by the unfettered use of all the powers that God has given to you."

To be an eagle in a hen run sounds so terribly sad. The eagle should be free, soaring up in the sky. That is what it was made to do. Some of us may be just like that – our potential unused, either because we are lazy or because of some false inferiority, unbelief or even fear. We do not have to be a grounded eagle. The secret, which really is not a secret, is to set out towards God determined to be a person of power, for no other reason than that it is what he intended for us.

Reading God's words, believing them and obeying could send us into a new life of freedom, but he must do the guiding and we must trust him to put the power into our "wings"!

***

Father, show me how I am missing out in the quality of life that your Son died to give me. May my desire for something more be met by your longing to see me "soaring".

Goodnight, Lord

11

And so I say to you: Ask, and you will receive; seek, and you will find; knock, and the door will be opened to you. For everyone who asks will receive, and he who seeks will find, and the door will be opened to anyone who knocks. Would any of you who are fathers give your son a snake when he asks for fish? Or would you give him a scorpion when he asks for an egg? Bad as you are, you know how to give good things to your children. How much more, then, will the Father in heaven give the Holy Spirit to those who ask him!

Luke 11:9–13

"Prayer", writes Reginald East in his book *When you Pray*, "is an adventure into God. We should therefore practise it as positively and with as much enthusiasm as we can."

Am I wrong in thinking that there is a subtle way of taking those words by suggesting that they could mean "if you have to do it, you might as well do it well"? I doubt that Reg East meant it in quite that way, but how many of us face the whole question of praying without some trepidation? We know that as Christians we have to pray, but real prayer which takes time, that is something different again.

Jesus, in his words on prayer, suggests that there should be perseverance in our praying, which in turn leads to the thought that prayer is something profound and vital to our Christian life. Reg East does not say that prayer is an adventure *with* God, but *into* God. In other words, prayer is approaching God and becoming absorbed in him, so that eventually there are no more words. Asking is comparatively easy as we bring our petitions to God. Seeking means an effort, even work, it is more difficult and takes time. Knocking speaks of decisiveness, of wanting to be let in and eventually entering in at the open door.

Prayer is asking, seeking and finding God, because in the end it is he whom our heart desires and only he can truly satisfy us. It may sometimes seem as if we are walking through the mist, even perhaps stumbling as we try to keep going, but we can know that God *is* there, and our eagerness to find him in this deep way can never exceed the eagerness of God that we should indeed meet. Prayer is talking to God and bringing him our needs, but more than that prayer brings us into God.

***

Lord, I see that the end of prayer is hallowed ground. Teach me the way into a life with yourself, give me the ability to persevere until I know something more of what prayer truly means.

Goodnight, Lord

12

And I prayed earnestly to the Lord God, pleading
with him, fasting, wearing sackcloth, and sitting in
ashes. I prayed to the LORD my God and con-
fessed the sins of my people. I said, "Lord God,
you are great, and we honour you. You are faithful
to your covenant and show constant love to those
who love you and do what you command. We
have sinned, we have been evil, we have done
wrong. We have rejected what you commanded us
to do and have turned away from what you
showed us was right . . .

"O God, hear my prayer and pleading. Restore
your Temple, which has been destroyed; restore it
so that everyone will know that you are God.
Listen to us, O God; look at us, and see the trouble
we are in and the suffering of the city that bears
your name." Daniel 9:3–5; 17–18a

"God does not pour out revival upon those who do not
seek it." These words were written by Ron MacDonald
and are at once an indictment and an encouragement.
All have not sought but we may seek.

Revival demands sacrifice on our part, and if we do
not see it it may be because we consider the sacrifice too
great. Revival demands repentance on a personal level
and on behalf of the nation. We may have to face up to
the searching of our hearts and lives, seeing what God
says about us and looking afresh at him.

We speak of having faith in God as if it is our faith which changes things. Only God can work, and if we do not believe that he *will* work then we shall not be interested in asking him. What we must be sure of doing is asking within his will, and being prepared for him to answer exactly according to what we ask.

In his book *Understanding Divine Healing* Richard M. Sipley tells of a blind woman who asked for prayer for a serious cold. This was all she wanted. Richard Sipley suggests that we should be specific about what we want and then ask for it.

What do you want today as you read this? A revival in your own life, a revival in the land? Daniel knew exactly what he wanted, he knew to whom he must turn and what he must do. He acknowledged God, and he acknowledged the wickedness and rebellion of the people, including himself. He pleaded and he fasted before God.

Is the price perhaps too much to pay?

Search me, Lord, and know my heart, and show me the way to serve you as you desire. Cause me to know myself without any deception and to withhold no part of myself from you.

Goodnight, Lord

13

O LORD, our Lord, your greatness is seen in all
   the world!
   Your praise reaches up to the heavens . . .
What is man, that you think of him;
   mere man, that you care for him?
Yet you made him inferior only to yourself;
   you crowned him with glory and honour . . .
O LORD, our Lord, your greatness is seen in all
   the world!   Psalm 8:1,4–5,9

Dr R. C. Sproul is an American theologian, and in his
book *The Holiness of God* he has written something
that has given me new light on the majesty of God.
Apparently when the word "Lord" appears in the
Scriptures in lower case letters the translator is indicat-
ing that the word *Adonai* is found in the Hebrew.
Adonai means "sovereign one". It is not the name of
God, it is a title for God. When LORD appears in
capital letters it indicates that the word *Jahweh* is used.
Jahweh is the sacred name, the unspeakable name, the
holy name, the name by which God revealed himself to
Moses in the burning bush. So, our psalm for tonight is
saying "O Jahweh, our Adonai, your greatness is seen
in all the world!"

LORD is the name of God. Lord is his title.

When we allow the meaning of what these words are
saying to sink deep into our mind it can open up a
whole new understanding of the awesome majesty and
holiness of our God.

Jesus has taught us to call God father, and as single entities, alone in the sense of living with ourselves, we know the comfort that our personal relationship with God, as father, brings to us. But as we turn our thoughts toward the God who is the Creator and upholder of all things, the God of the Old Testament, the God who is holy, the sense of familiarity is replaced by that of awe and reverential fear.

The holiness of God is the devastating light that appears to illumine every part of our being. In that light we know our worthlessness. Yet in a wonderful way we know that whilst God is holiness, he is also love, and in feeling condemned by the one, we are restored by the other.

Holy, holy, holy is your name, LORD, and your holiness causes my heart to worship . . .

Goodnight, Lord

14

To him who is able to keep you from falling, and to bring you faultless and joyful before his glorious presence – to the only God our Saviour, through Jesus Christ our Lord, be glory, majesty, might, and authority, from all ages past, and now, and for ever and ever! Amen.   Jude 24–25

In one edition of the Good News Bible these verses are headed "Prayer of Praise". If we divide the portion into two, we see that the first part talks about someone being able to do something. The second part describes this person.

We know that the words refer to God, and Jude is ending his letter, in which he encourages his readers "to fight on for the faith", with this paean of praise.

It seems to me to be impossible to read these words without a rush of joy – a feeling of exultation. Here is the underlining of God's ability and desire toward us, to bring us through each day, upholding us and working within us through the circumstances of our lives until the last day on earth has been lived and we eventually enter his presence. And what a presence! The presence of the one who has saved us and led and guided us, yes, but more than this: the presence of a mighty God, God of glory and majesty, a God of the past, a God of today and for ever. The glory of the Lord is something so great and wonderful that Moses was not allowed to see it (Exodus 33). The transfiguration of Christ with Moses and Elijah reminds us of the glory, and in the Book of Revelation are instances that reveal the glory of God.

We need sometimes to remind ourselves that we do indeed have a God who is our friend, but that he is also a God to worship, to stand before in wonder and in awe.

The very fact that he is such a God gives us the confidence for our earthly pilgrimage, the assurance that he is well able to keep us from falling, and does long to bring us faultless and joyful into his presence — working always to that end. A God to whom we may safely entrust ourselves!

Alleluia, Lord. You are worthy of praise and worship for yourself, yet you are my God and I am your child. Thank you.

Goodnight, Lord

15

It was about twelve o'clock when the sun stopped shining and darkness covered the whole country until three o'clock; and the curtain hanging in the Temple was torn in two. Jesus cried out in a loud voice, "Father! In your hands I place my spirit!" He said this and died. The army officer saw what had happened, and he praised God, saying, "Certainly he was a good man!" When the people who had gathered there to watch the spectacle saw what happened, they all went back home, beating their breasts in sorrow. All those who knew Jesus personally, including the women who had followed him from Galilee, stood at a distance to watch.   Luke 23:44—49

In the Old Testament we read that the High Priest could only enter the most Holy Place in the Temple once a year. This part was separated by a heavy curtain from the rest of the building. Once a year, the High Priest, making special preparations, was allowed to enter to make atonement for himself and for the people.

When Jesus became the sacrifice by his death on the cross, the curtain in the Temple was torn in two. The significance being that, from that moment of death, entry was opened up for all, not just one person, to enter into the "holy place" – God's presence.

The Scriptures tell us that we may "come boldly" – as beneficiaries from the death of Jesus we may now have a personal relationship with God. No longer is there anything between us, we need look to no other person, although Jesus in another sense was the High Priest and it is through him that we are free to come. These are things to ponder over, to remember with deep gratitude and thanksgiving. Our salvation is costly, and as we follow through the Old Testament to the New we see how God planned it and how all was wondrously fulfilled in the coming of his Son. It shows a love and care that sometimes we are tempted to doubt or disbelieve, but it is all gloriously true: God sent his son because he loved the world so much – and that includes you and me.

Thank you Father, for the love that has given me forgiveness and a new life with you. Thank you for a happy heart tonight as I joy in knowing you.

Goodnight, Lord

16

The Helper, the Holy Spirit, whom the Father will send in my name, will teach you everything and make you remember all that I have told you. Peace is what I leave with you; it is my own peace that I give you. I do not give it as the world does. Do not be worried and upset; do not be afraid.

John 14:26–27

In this chapter we twice have our Lord's words about being worried and upset. He is speaking to his disciples, and what he has to say is both puzzling and upsetting to these men who are his friends. Firstly, he is speaking to them after having just washed their feet; then they hear him say that he will be betrayed; he has confused Peter by telling him that he will deny knowledge of Jesus; and then he says that he is going away.

After all this he tells them not to be upset or to worry!

The gentleness and love of Jesus come through in these words, and they sound so very confident. How often have we said to someone, "Now, don't worry", when worry about the situation is gnawing away at our own heart?

Jesus knows, of course, that we do get worried and upset, sometimes about the silliest things. The reason we worry is because somehow we have lost control of the situation, the outcome is in the hands of someone else. It is as if we have no belief in ourselves any more.

Two things in these verses are linked to our Lord's

words. He says that the Holy Spirit will teach us, and that he gives us his own peace.

As Christians we are not alone, we have the Spirit of God within us, and if we will only listen to him he will prompt us when we need his help. The peace of God comes from the confidence we should have both of his presence and love, and his ability to help and guide.

The Holy Spirit is here called the Helper, which in turn means literally "someone who is called alongside". He is on our side, is our friend, our ally. His resources are infinite and he will, if we ask him, sort out that thing that so worries and upsets us. Whether it is big or small, he will set to work on our behalf.

✻✻✻

Lord, I do get anxious and upset, but just keep reminding me that you are in control of both the silly things that trouble me and the bigger things that cause me worry. Thank you that I need not be afraid for you are on my side.

Goodnight, Lord

17

Whoever goes to the Lord for safety,
   whoever remains under the
   protection of the Almighty,
can say to him,
   "You are my defender and protector.
   You are my God; in you I trust."
He will keep you safe from all hidden dangers
   And from all deadly diseases.
He will cover you with his wings,
you will be safe in his care;
   his faithfulness will protect and defend you.
You need not fear any dangers at night.

Psalm 91:1–5a

A little boy was leading his sister up a mountain path and the way was not too easy. "Why, this isn't a path at all," the little girl complained, "it's all rocky and bumpy." And her brother replied, "Sure, the bumps are what you climb on". These words are from *The Bumps are what you climb on*, a book by Warren W. Wiersbe, and to me they immediately encapsulate the Christian life. Believers find that the Christian path is not easy and can readily be likened to an upward mountain path. Trying to get to the top is a scramble with many a slip and slide, but it is true that you look for the bumps and rocky bits to find a foothold and move upwards.

The bumps and rocky bits on the Christian path are the things that help us go on – lift us higher. However, if we refuse to use the hard bits to help us climb, then we tend to take a very long time to move a short way. Although we all wear the masks that help to give the impression that everything is always well, there are times in everyone's life when there are problems. When things go against us we tend to complain or feel sorry for ourselves, even getting rather resentful.

The thing is to work through them, finding out why we feel as we do and then substituting a different emotion. God will answer our prayer for help and wisdom. Above all we should not brood on those things which cause us hurt and difficulty. As we learn to lift our hearts and minds to God so they can become less real or important. It is an encouragement to realize afresh that He knows about it all and understands our feelings, even when he is wanting us to move out of them.

✳✳✳

I realize that life has a million thorns to tear at me day after day but each one *can* be turned to an advantage. Help me to keep my eyes fixed on you, Lord, so that the problems of each day are minimized through your care.

Goodnight, Lord

18

Sing to the Lord, all the world!
   Worship the Lord with joy;
   come before him with happy songs!
Never forget that the Lord is God.
   He made us, and we belong to him;
   we are his people, we are his flock.
Enter the temple gates with thanksgiving,
   go into its courts with praise.
   Give thanks to him and praise him.
The Lord is good;
   his love is eternal
   and his faithfulness lasts for ever.

Psalm 100

There are plenty of times when we do not feel like shouting for joy to the Lord. Shouting maybe, when it seems that everything is going wrong, nobody cares and even God appears to have turned his back. How very easy it can be to become full of self-pity, and as day by day we do all of the things that have to be done, the waves ebb and flow in our innermost being and there is a veritable sea of resentment that builds up into a storm. That really is the moment when we have to look away from ourselves and try to concentrate a little on the Lord.

"Acknowledge that the Lord is God." Concentrate on the fact that he *is* God and then allow the thoughts to, as it were, play around that fact. Then widen out, rather as a stone is dropped into a pool, so that from there we go on to the next fact.

"He made us" – he made me. And if we are inclined to wonder why, the next phrase tells us: "We belong to him." Is there a warmth beginning to be felt inside as we ponder on the words that mean that we belong to him, that he made us? If we are as sheep in his pasture it means that he cares and looks after us.

Perhaps now is the moment to begin loving and praising him, to shout for joy, not for any other reason than that he is God – and that he made us and cares for us. Now we turn yet further away from ourselves and realize that the shout of joy is meant to come from all his people in unison. My shout of joy joins with yours, and ours joins with theirs, until wave after wave of praise rises from the hearts and perhaps from the mouths of his children right around the world. When we have realized all this perhaps we can sit quietly before him and really begin to come into personal contact with him. We begin to enter into temple gates, feeling now that we have the words of thanksgiving for what he has done and does, giving him praise as gradually we see that the darkness has gone. The Lord is good, he does not change, we vacillate but he is ever faithful, we can bow our heads and worship.

***

Father, I know that you love me and you will not let me go. Forgive me that I turn away and thus make myself miserable. Help me to keep my eyes fixed on you at all times, and to keep praising and worshipping.

Goodnight, Lord

19

Early the next morning the people went out to the wild country near Tekoa. As they were starting out, Jehoshaphat addressed them with these words: "Men of Judah and Jerusalem! Put your trust in the Lord your God, and you will stand firm. Believe what his prophets tell you, and you will succeed." After consulting with the people, the king ordered some musicians to put on the robes they wore on sacred occasions and to march ahead of the army, singing: "Praise the Lord! His love is eternal!" When they began to sing, the Lord threw the invading armies into a panic.

2 Chronicles 20:20–22

We have learnt much about praising God in recent years, although it seems strange that for so long Christians have failed to follow the Bible's many exhortations to praise him.

Noel Palmer in his latest book *Living Stones* writes that "Praise is a vote of confidence in God, whatever goes on around you".

Praise comes quite easily at some times – when we are with other Christians, when something wonderful happens, in fact, in all the good times. Certainly they can be wonderful times when our hearts – our whole beings – are lifted up in wonder and awe.

Praise when we are alone, perhaps in despair or loneliness, is not so easy. What are we supposed to praise about? The loneliness, the despair or the problems? No! We praise him because he is able to come into the loneliness. We praise him because he is the one who can resolve the problem.

Perhaps the reason that we go so long in our depressions, moods of self-pity and even resentment is because we petition God in the wrong way. Our petulant selfish prayers reflect our continual preoccupation with ourselves, when instead we should be more concerned with God, and with acknowledging him.

Noel Palmer continued writing about praise in his book by quoting Olive Wyon from her book *The School of Prayer*: "I have learned that whatever my circumstances may be, first of all I am not to ask . . . but always to adore!"

Praise is saying Yes. Despair is saying No. Despair suggests that there is no way out, no one to help. As Christians that is tantamount to denying our God.

Praise is an acknowledgement that God is, and our personal time alone with him creates that intimacy and fellowship that admits and believes that he is also our Helper, even when our immediate circumstances may be crushing us. In the end, too, the fact of praising reflects our true feelings for him.

✳✳✳

Lord, praise is not always easy, and yet by not praising you in all things I see that I am withholding that which is rightly due to your name. Create in me a thankful and praising heart that lifts me above my selfish thoughts and reveals the confidence and trust that I have in you.

Goodnight, Lord

20

So Jesus said again, "I am telling you the truth; I am the gate for the sheep. All others who came before me are thieves and robbers, but the sheep did not listen to them. I am the gate. Whoever comes in by me will be saved; he will come in and go out and find pasture. The thief comes only in order to steal, kill and destroy. I have come in order that you might have life – life in all its fullness.

"I am the good shepherd, who is willing to die for the sheep. When the hired man, who is not a shepherd and does not own the sheep, sees a wolf coming, he leaves the sheep and runs away; so the wolf snatches the sheep and scatters them. The hired man runs away because he is only a hired man and does not care about the sheep. I am the good shepherd. As the Father knows me and I know the Father, in the same way I know my sheep and they know me. And I am willing to die for them."   John 10:7–15

In the Bible, God's people are compared to sheep, and although as a quick thought this may not appear to be a compliment, sheep are gentle and peaceful animals. They are also, however, rather stupid creatures and do put themselves into danger. The shepherd is an important person to the sheep – he it is who watches out for them, guides them and makes sure that they have his protection. He leads them to water and food. Alone, sheep can have a hazardous time, falling perhaps and being unable to climb back on to safe ground.

The analogy of Jesus as our shepherd has always been a beautiful one. The good shepherd does know each of the sheep in his flock: the impetuous one, the timid one, the older, the young. Each is individual, and in looking after each one the shepherd takes all this into consideration.

Being a Christian is not easy, God needs us to be soldiers as in an army – obedient, ready to go forward, even to face the enemy. But he knows that we go forward trying to do his will with temperaments that are sometimes fearful, and prone to worry. Acknowledging this to ourselves and to God means that he can tend us as the shepherd does.

The timid sheep stays close to the shepherd; another will run off and get into trouble, but a call will bring the shepherd to his side to bring him back to safety. Tonight we may feel tired, weary, and even annoyed with ourselves over something that we wish either had not been done or should have been done. At the end of the day the shepherd checks the sheep, tends them. Our shepherd will do that for us, tending the wounds of the day, preparing us for the healing hours of sleep – if only we will let him.

Sheep can be silly, not always realizing all the good that the shepherd can do for them, missing out on his love and care.

***

Loving Shepherd, thank you for reminding me of all your care and provision. Help me to learn to follow you in trust at all times.

Goodnight, Lord

21

Whenever the people of Israel set up camp, Moses would take the sacred Tent and put it some distance away from the camp. It was called the Tent of the Lord's presence, and anyone who wanted to consult the Lord would go out to it. Whenever Moses went out there, the people would stand at the door of their tents and watch Moses until he entered it. After Moses had gone in, the pillar of cloud would come down and stay at the door of the Tent, and the Lord would speak to Moses from the cloud. As soon as the people saw the pillar of cloud at the door of the Tent, they would bow down. The Lord would speak with Moses face to face, just as a man speaks with a friend.   Exodus 33:7–11a

In *Best of Friends* Alec Thornhill writes about the enriching friendships that he has found in his life. In the last chapter he writes:

> I come finally to the realization that for me every friendship has become a three-cornered affair. Christ is the unseen Friend in every human relationship. As in Elgar's "Variations" there is an extra hidden melody, the Enigma, so in all the infinite variations on the theme there is the extra melody of Christ's own friendship – sometimes an enigma, but more often a living experience.

Friendship is a growing thing, from the first meeting, then the gradual moving on to greater knowledge of a person until there comes that more easy familiarity.

Now and again we meet someone with whom there is an immediate rapport, and within a few minutes a friendship is born. Some first meetings with Christ are like that, a conversion that is sudden and a relationship that gives immediately almost complete understanding of the new friendship. For others the growth is slower, but as times goes by so the friendship becomes deep and precious. What Alec Thornhill was also saying was that our human friendships are touched by the friendship that we have with Jesus.

Friends enjoy being with one another, doing things together, entering into each other's circumstances and problems. In its fullest meaning it is a two-way thing, each being sensitive to the other, giving and receiving.

In a Rolf Harris song, a little boy plans to visit Jesus in heaven and say "I'm Tommy . . . we talk all the time".

There is a happy give and take of chatter when we meet friends, then sometimes there are times of deeper discussion about personal affairs or even world affairs, and there are times when you just stay together in silence.

Happy remarks, deeper talks, or sometimes just being together in silence.

✳

Thank you for the friendship that has come out of your love and sacrifice for me. May all my human friendships be shared with you as we each seek to know you more.

Goodnight, Lord

22

What shall I bring to the Lord, the God of heaven, when I come to worship him? Shall I bring the best calves to burn as offerings to him? Will the Lord be pleased if I bring him thousands of sheep or endless streams of olive-oil? Shall I offer him my first-born child to pay for my sins? No, the Lord has told us what is good. What he requires of us is this: to do what is just, to show constant love, and to live in humble fellowship with our God.

Micah 6:6—8

Men, women and even children are involved in the hectic life style of today. Everything is done in a hurry, we chase from one thing to another. None of this is helped by what Christians consider their responsibilities apart from their everyday work.

Many a wife and mother not only looks after the home but copes perhaps with a job and a host of Christian activities. Her husband bears the strain and stresses of commuting, of his job, plus the men's meeting, the Parish Council or other similar church work.

Christian ministry, whether it be full-time or part-time, is only a part of the whole. Our Christianity is full-time, it should be our life, our way of living. Doing "things Christian" should slot normally into our lives and be undertaken because God wants us to do that particular thing. We are in danger of believing that the more we do, the better pleased God will be, whereas in

The Message from the Trees.
By the time these photos are
in full bloom so will your
faith be & your health & strength
ready & able for God to use ya

Thank you Lord.

Take this gift it's a diamond
it's never go~s to wearout
wee it, it might gie a wee bit
durty sometimes but just give
it a wee wash it will
care up Brand new every
time

fact he probably wishes that he could see a little more of us!

Does it happen like that in your family? The pattern of everyone going their different ways, and coming together only occasionally occurs, although each is doing something quite legitimately. Is this what God wants?

What does God require of us? Basically, he just wants us. He wants time with us. He does want us to serve him but in the way he chooses, and certainly not to the detriment of a life with him and with other members of our family.

Walking humbly with our God means looking to him, making sure that we are pleasing him. It does not mean setting ourselves in the position of thinking that we know best by working at things that we believe we *should* be doing.

Our God gives us the wonderful privilege of friendship — we spurn it when we turn our backs and concentrate on continually *doing* things.

✳✳✳

Cause me to know my priorities, Lord. Help me to serve you in the way which pleases you, in quiet companionship as well as in activity.

Goodnight, Lord

23

He always had the nature of God, but he did not
  think that by force he should
  try to become equal with God.
Instead of this, of his own free will he gave up all
  he had,
and took the nature of a servant.
He became like man
  and appeared in human likeness.
He was humble and walked the path of obedience
  all the way to death –
  his death on the cross.
For this reason God raised him to the highest place
  above and gave him the
  name that is greater than any other name.
And so, in honour of the name of Jesus all beings
  in heaven, on earth, and
  in the world below will fall on their knees,
  and all will openly proclaim
  that Jesus Christ is Lord,
  to the glory of God the Father.

Philippians 2:6–11

What does your name mean to you? Some people hate
their name and even change it, but our given name
really does become an absolute part of us, so much so
that sometimes our like or dislike of someone can stem
from another person we know who bears the same
name.

needed forgiveness may also forget about what was done. If this is too difficult we must then remind ourselves of how God has forgiven us, and this not just as his people, but on a personal level. It is on the basis of the death of Jesus, but once we claim forgiveness on the grounds of the Cross then God forgets about our sin.

He says that he blots them out (Isaiah 43:25) and that he will remember sins no more.

In Psalm 103 v. 12 we read, "As far as the east is from the west, so far does he remove our sins from us"; and in Jeremiah 31 v. 34b, "I will forgive their sins and I will no longer remember their wrongs."

If God, against whom we have and do sin so much, can forgive, dare we do less?

❋

May your presence in my life enable me to act at all times as you would act, forgiving and loving others that I may be freed to love you more.

Goodnight, Lord

25

As Moses lifted up the bronze snake on a pole in the desert, in the same way the Son of Man must be lifted up, so that everyone who believes in him may have eternal life. For God loved the world so much that he gave his only Son, so that everyone who believes in him may not die but have eternal life. For God did not send his Son into the world to be its judge, but to be its Saviour.

John 3:14–17

The children of Israel had a hard time wandering in the wilderness. As we read about their problems and their grumblings it is all so very much how we react today to the things that come into our lives.

So often we cry to God, he helps us and we go on, but somewhere things get rough again and we start murmuring once more.

The Israelites were journeying when suddenly it all got too much for them again. They began to murmur and get impatient. It is easy to imagine that something happened once too often for someone, and he or she exploded! "I'm fed up with this – I'm tired, there's no water, I'm hungry and I hate this food."

That was enough for the rest of the people, and they all started agreeing and grumbling to each other. The Scriptures tell us that they spoke against God and against Moses.

Retribution was swift. God sent poisonous snakes

among the people which bit them and they began to die. Quickly others came to Moses to ask for his help, acknowledging that they had been wrong. Moses prayed for the people, and God told him to make a bronze snake and put it high up on a pole so that those who were bitten could just look at the snake and then they would not die.

I suppose the words of John 3:16 are among the best-known in the world. Jesus spoke them to Nicodemus when he was explaining about his death, but we forget the picture that he gives in the previous verse. For the snake on the pole and the people looking and living is a picture of Christ dying on the Cross and people looking and believing.

Was it possible that there were some Israelites bitten and dying, knowing that all they had to do was to look at the bronze snake on the pole, and yet refusing to do so? The snake was a reminder of their sin. Perhaps there were some who obstinately refused to believe that they had done wrong and therefore would not look – and so they died.

And behind the truth of what Jesus was saying would happen to him is God's great love for the world. As he gave the children of Israel a way out, so the Cross is our way out from our sin – into life.

�֎

Thank you, Lord, that you caused my eyes to look at the Cross and understand. Thank you also, that this is where I can go when murmurings and grumblings overwhelm me. Thank you for the forgiveness and peace that comes from the death of Jesus.

Goodnight, Lord

26

Whoever does not carry his own cross and come after me cannot be my disciple. If one of you is planning to build a tower, he sits down first and works out what it will cost, to see if he has enough money to finish the job. If he doesn't, he will not be able to finish the tower after laying the foundation; and all who see what happened will laugh at him. "This man began to build but can't finish the job!" they will say. Luke 14:27–30

In some countries, instead of buying a house or apartment it is much more the thing to purchase a piece of land and then build a house on it, with building going ahead as money for it is available. This is why in some places half-built houses can be seen. Sometimes the family moves into just a room or two as they wait for the time when the house can be completed. There are often some lean years as all the resources are put into the building, but there is real satisfaction once all is finished.

However, inevitably there are some houses that are long in the building, and some that never get finished.

Without real determination that which has been planned is hard to follow through. So often, especially in the beginning of our Christian life, words frighten us, even God's words. "Taking up the cross" makes us think of agony, pain and blood, and perhaps we say to ourselves that this is a way that we cannot take, and so we carefully sidestep the issue and try to forget *that* Cross and the body that it carried.

What did Jesus mean when he spoke of carrying the cross? I don't think that he necessarily meant that there was going to be in any literal way the same agony that he suffered, although having said that, we know that some who have followed him have suffered and suffered greatly. But what he meant surely was that by taking up the cross we are taking up the Christian life and whatever is God's plan for us as an individual. At some point we decide to go his way, and whatever is on the path may bring pain or loneliness but it is all a part of the original decision. The determination to do his father's will did mean taking up the cross for Jesus, and if we are likeminded we too must be determined in our desire to follow and to do his will.

Just as the person who decides to build a house has to count the cost, so do those who weigh up whether or not to follow Jesus. At the start we mostly long to do so, whatever it is going to cost us. The pity is that sometimes as we go on we may think that the cost is too high. Jesus determined to go on to the end, and that was not for himself but for his friends, for us. If we will determinedly go to the end it brings its own reward, not only for the finish but because we have such company along the way. He has promised to be with us.

What pain or suffering comes from following you, Lord, may I bear with fortitude, safe in the knowledge that your presence will not leave me.

Goodnight, Lord

27

When Jesus returned to the other side of the lake, the people welcomed him because they had all been waiting for him. Then a man named Jairus arrived; he was an official in the local synagogue. He threw himself down at Jesus's feet and begged him to go to his home, because his only daughter, who was twelve years old, was dying.

As Jesus went along the people were crowding him from every side. Among them was a woman who had suffered from severe bleeding for twelve years; she had spent all she had on doctors, but no one had been able to cure her. She came up in the crowd behind Jesus and touched the edge of his cloak, and her bleeding stopped at once. Jesus asked, "Who touched me?" Everyone denied it, and Peter said, "Master, the people are all round you and crowding in on you." But Jesus said, "Someone touched me, for I knew it when power went out of me." The woman saw that she had been found out, so she came trembling and threw herself at Jesus's feet. There in front of everybody, she told him why she had touched him and how she had been healed at once. Jesus said to her, "My daughter, your faith has made you well. Go in peace." Luke 8:40–48

So often when we read Scripture, especially familiar passages, we only read the words. They give us a meaning of the passage, but what we fail to do is to use our imagination, to set the actual scene.

Our passage tonight paints a lively picture. The crowd of people are jostling and talking as they gather round Jesus. The sky is clear, the sun warm. A man begins to fight his way through the people, thrusting them aside as he makes for the one person he needs at this moment. Reaching him, he falls at the feet of Jesus. The whole mass moves forward as Jesus responds to the plea of Jairus to go to his daughter.

But in that crowd is someone else who is determined to reach Jesus. A woman moves forward through the people, not perhaps with the haste and passion of Jairus but nevertheless insinuating herself through until she too reaches Jesus. A desperate woman, for she has borne a chronic illness for twelve years. Thinking through what she was going to do, her faith led her to know that she only needed to touch him.

It was quite a shock when the man stops walking and asks who has touched him. Everybody is touching everybody else in that crowd, and Peter's tone when he spoke was bordering on impatience. Then everyone sees the frightened woman who comes forward and confesses what she has done. Then Jesus speaks just to her – and she has his peace.

✳✳✳

Thank you for reminding us that when I read of your days on earth it can seem very personal, because you are with me even as I read now. The words and experiences are all about somebody I know, and that makes me feel good.

Goodnight, Lord

28

He gave laws to the people of Israel
    and commandments to
    the descendants of Jacob.
He instructed our ancestors
    to teach his laws to their children,
    so that the next generation
    might learn them
    and in turn should tell their children.
In this way they also would put their trust
    in God
    and not forget what he has done,
    but always obey his commandments.
They would not be like their ancestors,
    a rebellious and disobedient people,
    whose trust in God was never firm
    and who did not remain faithful to him.
                Psalm 78:5–8

The verses in this psalm speak of what God did for the children of Israel in the wilderness, the way in which he helped them, worked miracles, continued to be with them. As the psalm continues we read of the details and remember all the ways in which God led his people.

God, as we say, bent over backwards to give them what they wanted. He sent them food when they grumbled, gave them water, protected them and led them. Yet still the people grumbled, still they rebelled against God.

Most of us have seen the child who, unable to have his own way, rants and raves, hitting out, feet stamping and shouting his hatred. As we grow up we learn self-control, but inside sometimes we may be like the child – hitting out at our circumstances, wanting things to be different from the way that they are.

The whole story of the journey through the wilderness by the children of Israel is a picture of our spiritual life here on earth. We are redeemed, and we set forth with God on our pilgrimage to heaven. He may give us many years and we have to accept the length of time, just as we have to accept what happens to us on the journey.

Many of us do rebel and grumble, but hopefully we do not let it be too long before we turn back to him. Perhaps one of the saddest phrases is in verse 32 of the Psalm: "in spite of his miracles they did not trust him".

In spite of all that he shows us of his love and personal care, it is possible to hurt him by a lack of trust, of not believing that he is for us, despite the times we have seen him working on our behalf. What do we need tonight to remind us of that love and his faithfulness? – the remembrance of the Cross, a special call perhaps, a miracle, some time when his voice was heard? He did not let us down when we specially needed his help.

✳✳✳

There have been so many times when your love and care has been manifested to me. May each one be as a stepping stone that leads me into a deeper knowledge and trust of you, my God and Saviour.

Goodnight, Lord

29

Jesus took the twelve disciples aside and said to them, "Listen! We are going to Jerusalem where everything the prophets wrote about the Son of Man will come true. He will be handed over to the Gentiles, who will mock him, insult him, and spit on him. They will whip him and kill him, but three days later he will rise to life."

But the disciples did not understand any of these things, the meaning of the words was hidden from them, and they did not know what Jesus was talking about.   Luke 18:31–34

The day came in the ministry of Jesus when, travelling with his disciples, he set his face towards Jerusalem. How early on he knew what was to happen to him there we do not know. Suffice it to say that at some period his Father must have told him what was going to take place.

Three times in Luke's gospel Jesus spoke about his death to his disciples, but they did not understand what he was trying to tell them. Jesus, however, knew it all and knew what it was going to cost. To face it he needed his Father's presence, and following his custom Jesus went to the Mount of Olives to pray.

On this night he asked that the cup of suffering should be taken away, but even as he asked, he reiterated his desire to do the will of his father. That was paramount, that he should fulfil God's purpose and plan for him. The rest we know.

His suffering was for us, he was about to die for a mass of people, alive and to come, who deserved nothing of him. He did it because God loved the world, and he was bonded to doing what God wanted of him, so he suffered and died. That death was for more than one thing. It paid a price for sin, it opened up an inheritance for God's children, it unleashed power and victory which we can appropriate today, and it revealed that the path God's son took must not be shirked by his followers.

Jerusalem, the place of suffering, may be very real to you tonight. It may mean pain, humiliation, shame or rejection. It meant all of these to Jesus, and he therefore knows what it costs us in heartache and suffering. His presence can bring a whole new dimension to the ability to carry on. Trusting him, talking to him, brings strength, courage and above all peace. God may open up difficult paths for us but he does not intend us to walk them alone. If we do then it is our own fault.

❊❊❊

Help me to accept all that you bring into my life, and to use everything as a means of drawing closer to you. Above all, keep me from the selfishness of grumbling, self-pity and resentment.

Goodnight, Lord

30

And he said to them all, "If anyone wants to come with me, he must forget self, take up his cross every day, and follow me. For whoever wants to save his own life will lose it, but whoever loses his life for my sake will save it. Will a person gain anything if he wins the whole world but is himself lost or defeated? Of course not! If a person is ashamed of me and of my teaching then the Son of Man will be ashamed of him when he comes in his glory and in the glory of the Father and of the holy angels. I assure you that there are some here who will not die until they have seen the Kingdom of God."   Luke 9:23–27

Over three hundred years ago a baby girl was born in France who eventually became Madame Guyon. Phyllis Thompson, the author of a recent biography of this lady, writes:

> The outward conditions of that young aristocrat living in the glittering reign of the Sun-king Louis XIV were vastly different from those of myself — but the inner experiences had a significance I could not ignore. True, some of them were quite beyond me, but if I could not understand them all, or the writer's interpretation of them, two spiritual principles emerged which I never forgot.
>
> One was accepting the will of God in the vicissitudes of life and the other the necessity of dying to self.

Madame Guyon's life was one of much suffering on every level, yet she accepted it all as from God and as a means of the death of self. She had the Scriptures and made them her constant reading, she knew the Holy Spirit, and she knew that life with God was lived in the inner self. These three things are of equal importance to twentieth-century Christians, as is the fact that Jesus said that we should take up the cross and follow him.

It can sometimes seem that the more comfortable life that we have today means that we seek also a more comfortable Christianity. The denial of self, the equating of our sufferings with those of Jesus, the acceptance of God's will are all things which are fundamental to our spiritual life, and yet we kick against them.

Whatever is in our life today needs to be accepted and worked out in the light of God's Word. Accepted, but more than that, used to refine and purify our nature until we become more like Jesus.

Our desire to know God should mean our acceptance of his will for *all* that comes into our life. It is in the sufferings and disappointments that he wants to teach us; refusal means a drawing back from him and a withering of the soul.

✳✳✳

If I cannot accept all that you bring into my life then I shall not grow spiritually. If I do not grow spiritually I shall not only have lost much, but denied you. Father, in your mercy hear my prayer for growth and the desire to accept and know your will in all things.

Goodnight, Lord

31

Lord, you are my God;
 I will honour you and praise your name.
You have done amazing things;
 you have faithfully carried out
 the plans you made long ago.
The poor and the helpless have fled to you
 and have been safe in times of trouble.
You give them shelter from storms
 and shade from the burning heat.

Isaiah 25:1,4

Isaiah was probably the greatest of the Old Testament prophets and his words are some of the most well known. These words though are words of confidence, and whoever had said them they would show a love and a strong belief in the One he called his God.

How strong is our desire to make known our faith in God? Are we able to praise him by using the words of Isaiah?

There are still many secret disciples, those who day by day mix with colleagues at work, attend coffee mornings, talk with neighbours, meet clients, who have never let it be known that they are disciples of Christ.

Many of us are just unable to talk about Jesus naturally, we keep the relationship with him a secret. It may well be that we are the type of person that holds things close, rarely speaking about the things that we hold very dear.

Our Lord understands these things because he made us, he knows the circumstances that have moulded us. He does not expect us to force ourselves into a role that is not ours, but he is prepared to give us the power and the words for the opportunities that present themselves. And if we really want to talk about him to people around us he will give those opportunities. He has promised us his Spirit to help, and if we only look to him we shall be able to do for him all the things that we might feel that we should.

But Isaiah's words, strong words, are words of exaltation and praise. They are words that – if we take and use them by saying them aloud, believing – will bring a warmth into our heart.

To acknowledge God as our God strengthens our faith, and pleases him. As we say the words we are acknowledging his hand on our life, not only at this moment but in what has happened in the past and also what will happen in the future, for he knows the end right through from the beginning. Sometimes we do not want to believe that he has allowed all that has come into our life. We may each be able to realize, though, that even in the darkest days we have learned something more of what it means to walk with God.

✳✳✳

"Lord, you are my God." Thank you for your love and care for me, as your child. Empower me to acknowledge you by word and deed in all the opportunities that are presented to me day by day. Forgive me for the times I have failed you today.

Goodnight, Lord

32

The Lord is my shepherd; I have everything I need. He lets me rest in fields of green grass and leads me to quiet pools of fresh water. He gives me new strength. He guides me in the right paths, as he has promised. Even if I go through the deepest darkness, I will not be afraid, Lord, for you are with me. Your shepherd's rod and staff protect me. You prepare a banquet for me, where all my enemies can see me; you welcome me as an honoured guest and fill my cup to the brim. I know that your goodness and love will be with me all my life; and your house will be my home as long as I live.

Psalm 23

The Twenty-third Psalm is one of the best-known passages of the Bible, and for many, the best-loved. The unfortunate thing about well-known verses of Scripture is that we sometimes look merely at the beauty of the words and miss the deep meaning behind them.

Tonight as you read this psalm, remember the one who wrote it. David had many problems during his life, and it may have been that in one of those times, possibly when he had to flee into the wilderness, he began to meditate on the Lord as a shepherd, remembering at the same time his own days of shepherding his father's flock. Everything in the psalm hinges on the first words, **The Lord is my shepherd.** If we cannot say those words in a personal way then the rest of the psalm cannot be appropriated. It is our relationship with the Lord that leads to the sort of trust manifested by David in the rest of the Psalm.

In the very first verse we read that knowing the Lord as shepherd means that we shall lack nothing. We can find rest in him, restoration, guidance, protection, freedom from fear.

Sheep need the help and care of the shepherd, and if we follow the analogy of ourselves as the sheep and Jesus as our shepherd, so do we need him. Each day can bring the circumstances and situations that cause us to wander away from the shepherd, or bring into our life something that makes us fearful or despairing.

It is knowing and holding on to a verse or passage from the Scriptures that will help to change our feelings about the situation. This psalm is one which reveals the care and love the shepherd has for us his sheep.

I was once walking in fields with a farmer's daughter. She saw a sheep lying on its back and I learned then what everybody who tends sheep knows, that the sheep cannot get up of itself. We went and rolled the sheep over so that it could stand up again.

Sometimes that is just how we are, absolutely cast down and unable to get up. This psalm reassures us that his caring extends to every part of us. What we feel and what we are, he can and will restore us. A good thought for the end of the day.

✳✳✳

Thank you for all that having you as my shepherd means. I look to you tonight for the cleansing and restoration that I need, that I may be renewed and healed in my innermost being and glorify you by all that I am.

Goodnight, Lord

33

You are like salt for all mankind. But if salt loses its saltiness, there is no way to make it salty again. It has become worthless, so it is thrown out and people trample on it. Matthew 5:13

We call ourselves followers of Christ, disciples, Christians. Should this make us different from those who are not?

Whatever commitment we have made presumably it was for a purpose. There was some need within us that could only be met by a decision to walk the Christian way and above all to walk it with the person of Christ himself. Having put a foot on the path we have gone on hopefully, learning more about this life with Christ with each mile that we have trodden.

It was to his disciples that Jesus spoke the words about the salt, and they are therefore words for us too, who are also his disciples.

Salt in food gives that something extra to the taste, it "lifts" the ingredients, and what is being eaten becomes exciting. Without it we are conscious that the food can be bland.

So, when Jesus applied these words to his followers, he was saying something very important. Salt is powerful, it is not neutral. Wherever it is used it makes a difference.

Jesus wants us to make a difference in the circumstances and situations in which each day we are immersed, he wants us to show that life as a Christian is different. It does not have to be by the spiritual content of our words, but by the way in which we speak the words of daily usage. It does not have to be by special deeds, but in the way we do each everyday task.

Everything we are, say or do should have that extra "something". The "something" which is like having salt in the soup as against leaving it out. Salt also preserves, it has a keeping power. Perhaps Jesus was suggesting that we must hold fast to the Christian truths that have been entrusted to us. We must learn from him all the time, so that we are of use. If we stop, grow weary in the Christian life, then gradually the "salt" in us becomes worthless.

Tomorrow is another day; a day of mixing with others and doing the many things that have to be done. A day of just being something for Christ.

✳✳✳

I realize that no special effort of mine will make me like you, Lord. It is only as I allow you to be seen in me that others will be aware of you. So may it be.

Goodnight, Lord

34

You have heard that it was said, "Love your friends, hate your enemies". But now I tell you, love your enemies and pray for those who persecute you, so that you may become the sons of your Father in heaven. For he makes his sun to shine on bad and good people alike, and gives rain to those who do good and to those who do evil. Why should God reward you if you love only the people who love you? Even the tax collectors do that! And if you speak only to your friends, have you done anything out of the ordinary? Even the pagans do that! You must be perfect – just as your Father in heaven is perfect!   Matthew 5:43–48

Someone once said in my presence that she felt her profession of Christianity did not mean very much, as she did not love her neighbour. It was only later that I wondered whether, in our sense of obligation to this commandment, we depend entirely on *feeling* love.

Because in our relationships with family and friends there are definite feelings and emotions which we call love, we assume that this has to be felt generally before we can say that we love our fellow human beings.

John Stott points out, in his commentary on the Sermon on the Mount, that "love . . . will be expressed in our deeds, our words and our prayers". So perhaps this is where we should start. Although we may not have enemies in the true sense of that word, there are those for whom we feel indifference, some whom we just cannot get along with, and others at work, church or as literal neighbours who on the surface seem determined to undermine us, or be less than helpful.

Our feelings of hurt pride and resentment in our dealings with such people merely feed the antagonism that we feel towards them. There has to be a definite determination to alter the situation.

In *Hidden Warfare* David Watson writes of a new missionary finding her senior colleague a problem. She daily read 1 Corinthians 13 and prayed for her fellow missionary. In a year the situation had radically altered. Prayer is probably the key to all such situations; not prayer for ourselves but prayer for the other person, endeavouring to discern his or her need. Then our words to them will become gentler, for this is a person for whom we have come before God. As actions are added we shall almost certainly find that rapport between us is growing.

Because we tend to run as far as possible from contact with those who are our "enemies", we deprive ourselves of working with God and disobey his command. To love those who love us means so little. To set out to love those who seem unlovable starts us out on a new path with the Lord.

✳✳✳

Lord, help me to face up to my lack of love for those around me whom I find uncongenial. Then teach me how to alter the situation.

Goodnight, Lord

35

The teachers of the Law and the Pharisees brought in a woman who had been caught committing adultery, and they made her stand before them all. "Teacher," they said to Jesus, "this woman was caught in the very act of committing adultery. In our Law Moses commanded that such a woman must be stoned to death. Now, what do you say?" They said this to trap Jesus, so that they could accuse him. But he bent over and wrote on the ground with his finger.

As they stood there asking him questions, he straightened himself up and said to them, "Whichever one of you have committed no sin may throw the first stone at her." Then he bent over again and wrote on the ground. When they heard this, they all left, one by one, the older ones first. Jesus was left alone, with the woman still standing there. He straightened himself up and said to her, "Where are they? Is there no one left to condemn you?"

"No one, sir", she answered. "Well, then," Jesus said, "I do not condemn you either. Go, but do not sin again." John 8:3–11

Jesus was well used to traps being set for him. Faced with the present situation he knew that if he agreed with the law the woman would have been taken away and stoned; if he disagreed, he himself would have been accused of not upholding the law.

His response was one that struck at the men before him. Jesus did not seek to say that the woman was innocent; his words to her were "Go, and do not sin again". He was implying that all her accusers were hypocrites, so quick to accuse and demand punishment, and yet each guilty in some way of having himself sinned.

It is so easy to make moral judgements, and where God's law is concerned we may need sometimes to stand firm and speak out, but how quickly we can become hypocritical. Personal attitudes, attitudes of groups, of churches, condemn without thought when scandal breaks, yet none of us is without sin. Are we in the crowd that storms for justice?

Jesus calmly looks at each one and gently says, "He who is without sin . . ." Faced with those words we can only turn away, like the men who came to him. Our sins may seem of little consequence, we can be hardened to our own ways of thinking and acting, but when we come face to face with the One who knows the heart of man our bravado diminishes like a pricked balloon and we can only slink away. For sin is sin. Lying and cheating are as bad as adultery – we cannot grade sin.

✳✳✳

Father, help me to see situations through your eyes and to act as Jesus would. Enable me to be honest with myself and to show true love in my attitude to others' shortcomings and sin.

Goodnight, Lord

36

Submit yourselves to one another because of your reverence for Christ.

Wives, submit to your husbands as to the Lord. For a husband has authority over his wife just as Christ has authority over the church; and Christ is himself the Saviour of the church, his body. And so wives must submit completely to their husbands just as the church submits itself to Christ.

Husbands, love your wives just as Christ loved the church and gave his life for it. He did this to dedicate the church to God by his word, after making it clean by washing it in water, in order to present the church to himself in all its beauty — pure and faultless, without spot or wrinkle or any other imperfection. Men ought to love their wives just as they love their own bodies. A man who loves his wife loves himself.   Ephesians 5:21–28

"Last Sunday Mary wasn't well, so I got the children up and out to church so that she could rest. In the past I would have made her get up, but I'm learning to be more considerate."

These words, written in a recently published book, gave me a jolt, perhaps because I had thought that the new generation of married couples had come to terms with each other as individuals, especially when they are Christians.

We would be forgiven for thinking that older men might look on marriage in a different light; they were brought up to think that wives are there to make life smooth in the home!

This passage of Paul's in his letter to the Ephesians may read harshly, but in fact it throws up the possibility of a gentle, loving, considerate relationship between two people, where headship does not mean authoritarianism but being the spokesman and final arbitrator. Demands and orders have no place in partnership, and submission is a yielding to another, not stark obedience without discussion.

Our reading commences with the injunction that we all should submit to one another, with the following verse merely reminding us that this must also happen in the home. As individuals we each have our space and worth in the world. We each have the right to give our point of view, whether in a church, work or home situation. Love should be the keynote which brings with it consideration for the other person, and an understanding of their circumstances.

Perhaps the end of this day is a time to evaluate our relationships and our attitudes to one another. Marriage partnership may not really be a partnership but just two people loving and living together, with one so dominant that the other is expected to "obey".

Possibly we could take a new attitude into a situation or into any place where we work with others.

✳✳✳

Please reveal to me where I tend to put myself forward and fail to show consideration and love to others.

Goodnight, Lord

37

The LORD is my shepherd.
  I have everything I need.
He lets me rest in fields of green grass
  and leads me to quiet pools
  of fresh water.
He gives me new strength.
He guides me in the right paths,
  as he has promised.
Even if I go through
  the deepest darkness,
  I will not be afraid, LORD,
  for you are with me.
Your shepherd's rod and staff
  protect me.

Psalm 23:1–4

Death is something that we each have to prepare for, for it comes to each one of us. When we are young death seems far away, and it can be many years before it touches us in any way.

Personal preparation should entail understanding of why we are on earth, what the journey is about, and where we shall be after death. If we know that our ultimate destination is heaven that can take away fear. And if there is still fear we should examine it before God and allow him to minister to us concerning it.

But if we need to prepare ourselves for death we need

also to prepare for the death of those close to us. This should be not in a morbid fashion but realistically. Most children will lose parents, one of a married couple will go first; keeping our minds closed to this will make the event even worse when it eventually comes.

These times will indeed be "the deepest darkness", but again we are assured that our Lord will be with us. We must be prepared to grieve, yet determine also to seek and stay close to him whilst we do so. Our grieving shows the worth to us of the person who has died, an acknowledgement of the gap left in our lives. We are not meant to be stoics, but we are meant to make sure that when we go through our "dark places" we go with the Lord. He does not mean us to go through them believing that we are alone. Acknowledging his presence will bring the sense of his support and his shepherding.

Father, when I walk through my dark places help me to realize your presence with me.

Goodnight, Lord

38

Jesus went on into Jericho and was passing through. There was a chief tax collector there named Zacchaeus, who was rich. He was trying to see who Jesus was, but he was a little man and could not see Jesus because of the crowd. So he ran ahead of the crowd and climbed a sycamore tree to see Jesus who was going to pass that way. When Jesus came to that place, he looked up and said to Zacchaeus, "Hurry down, Zacchaeus, because I must stay in your house today."

Zacchaeus hurried down and welcomed him with great joy. All the people who saw it started grumbling, "This man has gone as a guest to the home of a sinner!"

Zacchaeus stood up and said to the Lord, "Listen, sir! I will give half my belongings to the poor, and if I have cheated anyone, I will pay him back four times as much."

Jesus said to him, "Salvation has come to this house today, for this man, also, is a descendant of Abraham." Luke 19:1–9

I know of a superior cat who is named after Zacchaeus – because he climbs trees. Isn't it true that we remember Zacchaeus because he was short, he wanted to see Jesus and he climbed a tree to do so?

It is a lovely story and the Good News Bible text makes it especially vivid. As we imagine the scene we can only conjecture as to why Zacchaeus wanted so much to see Jesus, but there is nothing to suggest that it was anything more than curiosity.

That reminds me of how easy it is for us as Christians to stop others seeing Jesus. Occupied even with our own desire to be close to him, we can forget others outside the circle who may want to know him. Zacchaeus had his own solution. Determined, he ran and climbed a tree alongside the route that Jesus was taking, and he saw him! But Jesus also saw Zacchaeus, and he knew him; knew all about him, knew that he was a tax collector and all that meant, but he also saw something of what perhaps Zacchaeus himself was not consciously aware of, his need " . . . I must stay in your house today". To those in the crowd Zacchaeus was an outcast – the chief of tax collectors, Jews who served the Roman Government and defrauded their own people. And this Jesus wanted to visit him in his home!

For Zacchaeus the meeting was wonderful. Perhaps it was the first time for a long period that someone, apart from his own kind, had voluntarily suggested coming to his home. What it did was to make him face his sin. Immediately he offered restitution – four times was almost the full requirement of the law in the case of theft. Over and above it he intended giving half his possessions to the poor. This is a complete picture of salvation. The need of man, the recognition of sin, faith in Jesus and a new relationship with him.

✳✳✳

Help me, Lord, to keep the joy of belonging to you fresh in my heart and to seek to obey you in all things.

Goodnight, Lord

39

Be my secure shelter
  and a strong fortress to protect me;
  you are my refuge and defence.
You have taught me ever since I was young,
  and I still tell of your wonderful acts.
Now that I am old and my hair is grey,
  do not abandon me, O God!
Be with me while I proclaim your power and might
  to all generations to come.
Your righteousness, God, reaches the skies.
  You have done great things,
  there is no one like you.

Psalm 71:3,17–19

What a mixture our thoughts and moods are sometimes. Here in our passage is a cry for help, and then, later, words of confidence and praise. Isn't that how we sometimes feel? The downward plunge of our spirits that causes a sense of darkness and a chaos of thinking; the insecurity that can come with old age, even though security is all around us. The slough of despond looms at our feet, and our heart cries out silently for hope and help.

It is a time to remember the faithfulness of God; a time to appreciate the weakness and frailty of man. Loneliness, dark moods, sadness, are stepping stones to realizing anew the greatness of God, a God who never abandons his child, who cares not about length of years or whiteness of hair. Nothing of this alters the relationship, as well the writer of this psalm knows, and as we also know when once more we face things in a practical way.

All God's resources are as much ours today as they have ever been. We can think back on the many times when he has come to our rescue, has carried us, has seen us through dark periods. We can remember the times of joy, the episodes of closeness and glorious light, the number of times of blessing. Nothing has changed — he is the same God who spoke to us in our youth, who led us out, taught and empowered us. He is still ready to lead us on, to help us to grow spiritually, and to see afresh the wonder of his love and the power of his salvation.

Within us is the same person who first heard the voice of God, and it is with that same person that God goes on wanting to communicate.

Indeed, we can praise him, and in praise the darkness will miraculously turn to light. We shall feel strength returning so that we know that we are precious to him and will always be so until we meet him face to face.

⁂

How good it is to remember your faithfulness over the years, Lord. I know that you will not abandon me, and that I am safe in your care.

Goodnight, Lord

40

Finally, build up your strength in union with the Lord and by means of his mighty power. Put on all the armour that God gives you, so that you will be able to stand up against the Devil's evil tricks. For we are not fighting against human beings but against the wicked spiritual forces in the heavenly world, the rulers, authorities, and cosmic powers of this dark age. So put on God's armour now! Then when the evil day comes, you will be able to resist the enemy's attacks and after fighting to the end, you will still hold your ground.

Ephesians 6:10–13

Our relationship with God grows day after day as we seek to know him more. This relationship can be built up in two ways, by what we learn from him in the silence of communication, and by the circumstances of the happenings of each day.

Our reaction to the detail of daily events will spring from knowledge of God and his ways, and this knowledge comes from reading the Bible, praying and listening to God, reading about the experiences of other Christians, and generally always remaining open to spiritual things.

In this passage Paul is seeking to give advice on the way that as Christians we must be prepared to deal with the unseen world. The Devil is totally opposed to God and his purposes, therefore he is also against all believers. As Paul is writing about a battle it is easy for him to suggest the analogy of Christians as soldiers who should be prepared for the fight. Our strength and power is found in God, and all parts of the accoutrement come from our stand in him.

Truth, righteousness, knowledge of the Gospel, faith, salvation are all defences against the enemy. The one offensive weapon is a sword, which is the Word of God, and we learn how to use it from Jesus's example in the desert (Matthew 4).

Where do we find our enemy? He seeks to wound and defeat us through the mind when we doubt God, when we allow self-pity to engulf us, when resentment sours us, when we allow temptation to turn into sin. These can all overcome us as we react to people or events each day. Although we can scoff at the idea of deliberately putting on the armour piece by piece each morning, we do need to be protected by a knowledge of the truth of what Paul is saying and a recognition of the wicked spiritual forces that lie in wait.

Through prayer we can play our part in the conflict that affects not only individual believers but world events. Much of what we see going on around us is a part of Satan's strategy. Our prayer adds to the strength of God's side.

✳✳✳

Thank you for the reminder of the warfare in which, as a believer, I must be a part. Keep me strong and prepared to recognize the wiles of the Devil in my own life, and in the greater events around me. Teach me how to pray.

Goodnight, Lord

41

Well, whatever you do, whether you eat or drink, do it all for God's glory. Live in such a way as to cause no trouble either to Jews or Gentiles or to the church of God. Just do as I do; I try to please everyone in all that I do, not thinking of my own good, but of the good of all, so that they might be saved.   1 Corinthians 10:31–33

I read recently that Roman Catholics tend to use the word "evangelization" as meaning "living and speaking and working in such a way that the light of the Gospel is shed into every aspect of life". Non-Roman Catholics would use the word to describe the proclamation of the Gospel.

Those who believe in Christ need to proclaim the Gospel, but how vital it is also to make our Christian belief a total part of our living. Our actions and way of life must back up what our lips say. However earnest we may be in wanting to tell others about Jesus Christ and what relating to him means, if the way we live our lives is at variance with our words then our listeners will not heed us.

"Living" means the way in which we conduct our life, the way in which we relate to others, whether family, friends, acquaintances or strangers. Our reactions, our manners, the whole structure of our life must not only be based on Christian principles but permeated by the love of God. We are ambassadors for Christ, acting for him, doing as he would. "Speaking" means that our words should be harmonious – when we speak of him we should know how to tell about God's love and what Jesus has done for us, when we speak of ordinary things others should be able to tell by our manner that there is something different about us.

"Working" does not just mean teaching in Sunday School, or preaching or working with a Christian organization. It means that if we do those things they link up with whatever else we do, the home tasks or all that we term work. For whatever we do, we should do it well because we belong to Christ.

✳❋✳

May all I do always glorify you, Lord, and cause others to see you.

Goodnight, Lord

42

As Jesus and his disciples went on their way, he came to a village where a woman named Martha welcomed him in her home. She had a sister named Mary, who sat down at the feet of the Lord and listened to his teaching. Martha was upset over all the work she had to do, so she came and said, "Lord, don't you care that my sister has left me to do all the work by myself? Tell her to come and help me." The Lord answered her, "Martha, Martha! You are worried and troubled over so many things, but just one is needed. Mary has chosen the right thing, and it will not be taken away from her."   Luke 10:38–41

Mary and Martha lived in Bethany, a small village near the south-eastern base of the Mount of Olives, and barely two miles' walk from Jerusalem. Jesus had found a welcome here in the home of the two sisters and their brother Lazarus. We are told that He loved "Martha and her sister and Lazarus" (John 11:5)

Martha, perhaps the most forceful and practical of the three, may well have been the eldest, and it was she who ran the home. Her brother and sister seemed to have been quieter in temperament. This vignette tends to uplift Mary whilst rebuking Martha, but perhaps we see it in too black-and-white a way.

We all have different temperaments. Some of us *are* quiet and thoughtful, others of us *are* quick. Even in our own families we find that the members do not do things in the same way, there are the dreamers and the doers, and there are times when it is difficult to tolerate each other because of these differences.

However, we do have to have the dreamers, the introverts, people who thoughtfully work things through. We need, too, the practical folk, those who get on with things. Jesus loved Mary, the gentle spirit who wanted to be with him, the person who sought to learn from him – but Jesus also loved Martha. She may have had more problems, she may not have devoted so much time to their friend, but she was loved.

Some of us find the Christian life difficult, and then it seems that there are those who are endued with so much that makes it all seem so easy. What Jesus said to Martha she would have taken to heart, and the words would have gone deep inside her.

In fact, whether we are a Mary or a Martha we each need Jesus, and once we belong to him he will teach us, doing his own work in our lives. It is not that we shall be transformed into a totally different type of person, but we shall be refined, our priorities will change, we shall understand each other better.

"Jesus loved Martha and her sister and Lazarus."

I am what I am, Lord, but I want to be what you want me to be. Thank you for the assurance of your love and your refining process in my life.

Goodnight, Lord

43

Dear friends, let us love one another, because love comes from God. Whoever loves is a child of God and knows God. Whoever does not love does not know God, for God is love. And God showed his love for us by sending his only Son into the world, so that we might have life through him. This is what love is: it is not that we have loved God, but that he loved us and sent his Son to be the means by which our sins are forgiven.

We love because God first loved us.

1 John 4:7–10,19

"We love because God first loved us." God *is* love. He is in the love that surrounds us, and it is his love that draws us to him. We are his creation, and this too is something that underlines and strengthens our realization of his love.

Out of God's love for us comes our response, and we have love not only for him but for others. We have love, because of the love that God has for us. The knowledge and realization of his love for us causes the response, and as we think of how his love is manifested we remember afresh that he gave his Son, and sent him to live in the world that he had created. Sent him, because by doing so he could really show how much his creation meant to him. John 3:16 says it all – a love so great that God became man in order to save mankind.

We tend to forget that our need of a Saviour was so

great. We may even fail to understand fully why God himself was the only one who could save us. However, the one who is owed is the only person who can absolve the debt.

Our sin and separation from God could only be healed by God himself, and it is a measure of his love that it was accomplished. Again, we cannot fully comprehend all that it meant for Jesus to walk this earth for thirty-three years, or to face the indignity, humiliation and pain of a trial and death on a cross.

"He died that we might be forgiven", says the children's hymn. We could also say that he died because of God's love for us.

Our response to God's love is to reciprocate it, to love him because he loves us. Yet there is something else: loving God means that we have to love one another. John reminds us that if we love God then we must also love our brother and sister. That is the real test of our love for God.

❋

It was your love that drew me to yourself, Lord. May that love be seen and given to those whom I meet tomorrow and every day.

Goodnight, Lord

44

My Father's glory is shown by your bearing much fruit; and in this way you become my disciples. I love you just as the Father loves me; remain in my love. If you obey my commands, you will remain in my love, just as I have obeyed my Father's commands and remain in his love.

I have told you this so that my joy may be in you and that your joy may be complete. My commandment is this: love one another, just as I love you.   John 15:8–12

More and more I become aware of how precious each one of God's children is to him. It may take some time for us to recognize his love for each one of us personally. We tell ourselves that we are not very lovable, our faults are many, we keep failing.

We know that he is love, and that he loves us; but it can seem that he loves his people *en masse* rather than that he loves and rejoices in us as individuals. Have we ever thought that if this were really the case he would have made us all the same? I think that he likes our individuality, the things that make us different from each other, for he does not treat us all in the same way. Here I am not referring to our outward circumstances, but to the way he teaches us about himself.

God responds to the "bubbly" person in a way suited to his or her temperament, whereas the more introverted know him in a different way. Yet no temperament makes him impatient, because we belong to him and he deals with us as we are. To me that reveals real love.

It also makes me conscious of having to try to respond to those around me and to love them in that same way. This means not continually getting irritated by attitudes, but trying to understand how people feel, and above all realizing that they too, as Christians, are trying to respond to God working in their lives just as I am. Their experiences will not be the same as mine simply because we are different, and God is dealing with us differently. So I must not be despondent if others tell of experiences that differ from mine, nor exalt if I feel that I have had a special revelation. We are all learning from God and from each other, and my attitude of love and encouragement to others should be the same as God's to me.

I enjoy learning from you, Lord – keep me aware of your Holy Spirit's promptings so that I quickly understand what you are teaching me.

Goodnight, Lord

45

Give thanks to the Lord,
　because he is good;
　his love is eternal.
Give thanks to the greatest of all gods;
　his love is eternal.
Give thanks to the mightiest of all lords;
　his love is eternal.
He alone performs great miracles;
　his love is eternal.
By his wisdom he made the heavens;
　his love is eternal;
he built the earth on the deep waters;
　his love is eternal.
He made the sun and the moon;
　his love is eternal;
the sun to rule over the day;
　his love is eternal;
the moon and the stars to rule over the night;
　his love is eternal.

Psalm 136:1–9

"It is a good practice to look back at the end of each day at all the things that have given you pleasure or satisfaction and turn to God in gratitude." So writes Christopher Bryant.

The very fact of trying to put this into practice means that we have to find God in the happenings of the day.

The more we see him in the different situations the stronger does our sense of thanksgiving grow until we truly realize his hand and his presence throughout our day. Then the mind takes over, to put into words our praise, and then the heart – or feelings – and we find that gratitude and love flow from us.

So many things appear in our day that can make us grateful. The fact that we have food when we are hungry, that our home brings us pleasure, that we have warmth when it is cold. We may have seen something of beauty, or accomplished something that is a cause of satisfaction. There may have been a new moment of understanding with a colleague or a family member. Or perhaps there was something that reminded us overwhelmingly of God's care.

It is worth going over the day to make ourselves aware of all that came into it, and to be reminded of God's love. Our own love will respond to his as we pray, and the more we pray the more it fosters the growth of love.

Our thanksgiving expresses our faith in God as we acknowledge his presence in all the events of the day.

Thank you, Father, for all the good things that have been a part of my day.

Goodnight, Lord

46

For this reason we have always prayed for you, ever since we heard about you. We ask God to fill you with the knowledge of his will, with all the wisdom and understanding that his Spirit gives. Then you will be able to live as the Lord wants and will always do what pleases him. Your lives will produce all kinds of good deeds, and you will grow in your knowledge of God. May you be made strong with all the strength which comes from his glorious power, so that you may be able to endure everything with patience. And with joy give thanks to the Father, who has made you fit to have your share of what God has reserved for his people in the kingdom of light.   Colossians 1:9–12

In the biography of E. M. Blaiklock, *A Christian Scholar*, we read that when he was dying of cancer a friend asked him, "Well, what about beyond death?" and Blaiklock replied, "My greatest hope is reunion with Kathleen [his wife] but over and above that I want to hear from God that my life has been worthwhile."

As we go through life we find that inevitably it falls into different periods – before starting work, after marriage, when the children came, the landmarks of reaching thirty, forty or retirement. Sometimes we stop and think of what we have done in our lifetime, and it appears to be very little. It has just been a case of going on each day until the days have lengthened into years.

I suspect that most of us would like to have been chosen by God to do something spectacular, or at least to do something different. Our dreams would not be dreams if they did not outstrip the possible! But a life worthwhile in God's eyes does not necessarily mean that it must be one made up of great deeds. In fact, many of us don't have the time for doing much – a mother with young children to look after can only think of their needs and those of the home; a working Mum has even more cares. A man is often caught in the treadmill of daily work and earning a living.

Professor Blaiklock was an exceptional man, a classical scholar and author of many books; but he was not thinking of his learning, his teaching or his writings when he spoke those words. I am sure that he was more concerned with whether the way he had lived his life had pleased God, because only then could it be termed worthwhile.

It is not necessarily the things that we do that are so important, but how and why they are undertaken.

Pleasing God is really the most important thing, and that means staying very close so that firstly we know what he wants of us, in the place where he has put us, and, secondly, that we let him teach us.

Maybe it is worth thinking about what a life worthwhile to God really is, and what it means in our situation.

✻

Father, I do want my life to be worthwhile. If I have in any way gone off course please show me the way back, and help me to serve you loyally and cheerfully in all that you want me to do.

Goodnight, Lord

47

Put yourself to the test and judge yourselves, to find out whether you are living in faith. Surely you know that Christ Jesus is in you? – unless you have completely failed. I trust you will know that we are not failures. We pray to God that you will do no wrong – not in order to show that we are a success, but so that you may do what is right, even though we may seem to be failures. For we cannot do a thing against the truth, but only for it. We are glad when we are weak but you are strong. And so we also pray that you will become perfect.

2 Corinthians 13:5–9

At the end of a day we can feel at peace with ourselves or we can feel that we have muddled through the day, and not be too clear as to what has actually been accomplished. One of the things that we should be prepared to do in life is to understand ourselves, to come to terms with the way in which we act and react and how we tackle our work. Many of us work ourselves far too hard, everything that comes to hand has to be done by ourselves, just as if we had never heard of the word "delegation".

We may be so disorganized that the end of the day finds us exhausted and with the realization that little has actually been done. It is so easy for a busy wife and mother to dash from task to task without actually planning the day, feeling rushed and harassed, unable to find real time for the members of the family because of the feelings of having so much to do.

The day is not given to us just to get through in whatever way we can. It is not a matter of getting up in the morning and somehow managing to reach bedtime. If this is what it feels like then we need to ask ourselves why? Reaching some sort of answer should enable us to find a way out and to make the quality of our life better.

Often we struggle along because we feel that we have to *do* things. In his letter to the Corinthians Paul suggests that they judge – or examine – themselves. We sometimes need to do that – to see that we are not living life in our own way, striving at work, hassled at home, but making sure that we are truly living in faith, that we allow our Lord to enter into every part of our life. We should surrender everything to him, and not think that there are matters that we need to manage ourselves. As we hand over the In-tray to him, we will enable him to show us how to cope with the day – breakfast times and getting down to work, our problems hour by hour – so each day will be a day truly lived with Jesus.

***

I acknowledge my desire to do my own thing in so many situations. Help me to hand everything over to you, that together we may cope with what each day holds.

Goodnight, Lord

48

Do not be afraid – I will save you.
  I have called you by name – you are mine.
When you pass through deep waters,
  I will be with you;
  your troubles will not overwhelm you.
When you pass through fire, you will not be burnt;
  the hard trials that come will not hurt you.
For I am the LORD your God,
  the holy God of Israel, who saves you ...
because you are precious to me
  and because I love you and give you honour.
Do not be afraid – I am with you!
  From the distant east and the farthest west,
  I will bring your people home.

Isaiah 43:1b–3a,4b–5

Fear is corroding, it eats away at our innermost being; it enters into so much of our lives. We know that the Lord understands how fear attacks us because so often he bids us not to be afraid. In his love he seeks to reassure us of his care.

The opposite of faith, fear is spiritually weakening and is a denial of God's protection and love. Mere words will not convince us, but if we daily seek to understand more about God's love and his ways with those he has redeemed, we shall find our trust deepening.

We need to take to ourselves God's assurance that we are precious to him; to meditate on the manifestation of love through the coming to earth of his Son as Saviour. We may be confident because of our relationship with our Father, and we can look to him for his assistance and guidance.

If we are parents we can understand something of the trust that we hope our children will have in us. We want to give them the security that will help and support them. We want to do our best for them. We should grieve if we thought that they would not turn to us, yet we are human beings and possibly fallible in our relationships. God, however, is neither and he has promised us so much. The very fact that he says that he is with us means we can be sure that he is. But even more than dependence on his words is the fact that we can rely on the nature of God. Who he is gives credence to what he says.

Every day gives the opportunity of facing whatever it is we fear and exchanging it with faith in a God who is ever faithful to us. The more we set out to know him the more we shall realize how greatly he loves us.

❋

I will trust in you, my God, and not be afraid.
Cause my heart to rest quietly in you.

Goodnight, Lord

49

We know that in all things God works for good with those who love him, those whom he has called according to his purpose. Those whom God had already chosen he also set apart to become like his Son, so that the Son would be the first among many brothers. And so those whom God set apart, he called; and those he called, he put right with himself, and he shared his glory with them.

In view of all this, what can we say? If God is for us, who can be against us? Certainly not God, who did not even keep back his own Son, but offered him for us all! He gave us his Son – will he not also freely give us all things?

Romans 8:28–32

We know says Scripture very definitely, but I wonder if we all truly believe in our hearts that good comes out of all that happens. We may be certain of our love for God but find it very difficult actually to see a form or a continual good in our lives.

It does, of course, depend on what we mean by good. We can only become disillusioned if we believe that it means having wealth or having our own way. It means facing the disappointments, assimilating the hurts, bearing periods of frustration. It can mean coping with death and altered life styles, loss of work, or children leaving home. It may mean a restricted life style or having to live alone. It is not the circumstances that are necessarily good, but the result of them in our lives and the working out of the acceptance of them.

With all this we may link those wonderful words "If God is for us, who can be against us?" If God is for us whatever our circumstances, and we accept wholeheartedly the knowledge of his love and care, then everything must work out for good. Not the "good" of rewards or ease, but the "good" that conforms us to the likeness of his Son. For that is our calling. God's intention is that we shall be like him.

So the circumstances of today, whatever they may be, are not of no avail. The hurts and the joys are all a part of growth, and the more we understand that he is using them for our good the easier will be our dependence and trust.

God is on our side – he is for us – and the argument is that, if he gave his Son for love of us, will he not see that we go through to the fulfilment of his plan?

✳

Thank you for my position in Christ. May I understand more fully your desire to work in and through my life, that you may be glorified.

Goodnight, Lord

50

I will always thank the LORD;
  I will never stop praising him.
I will praise him for what he has done;
  may all who are oppressed listen and be glad!
Proclaim with me the LORD's greatness;
  let us praise his name together!
Psalm 34:1–3

Giving praise to the Lord is for the dark times and for the joyful times. David did not have an easy life and yet we find that mingled with his cries for help and in the midst of disaster, he could still praise his God.

In this psalm David gives us a picture of God's ways. It is a testimony of how he has proved God in his life, and he starts it by giving praise.

It is an extraordinary thing, but when we use some of the psalmist's words of praise or our own, our heart seems to lighten. What happens is that for a few moments we forget ourselves and our problems, and our minds are concentrated on God. We do not have to think of reasons why we should praise him; we allow our lips to voice his greatness and our mind realizes his pre-eminence. Then gradually we can meditate on his love and provision, and praise him afresh for his plan of salvation, our forgiveness and inheritance. Praise acknowledges all that God is and who he is. When we fail to praise him we are failing to give him his due, and at the same time we are ourselves diminished.

Therefore praise should be continually on our lips and in our hearts, lifting us at difficult times as it did David, but always acknowledging God. We should praise him when we feel like it and when we do not, for praise, in a way, is a sign of spiritual maturity. The more we know God the more we will want to praise him.

May praise be on my lips and in my heart continually as I acknowledge your greatness.

Goodnight, Lord

51

I call to you, LORD; help me now!
  Listen to me when I call to you.
Receive my prayer as incense,
  my uplifted hands as an evening sacrifice.
LORD, place a guard at my mouth,
  a sentry at the door of my lips.
Keep me from wanting to do wrong
  and from joining evil men in their wickedness.
May I never take part in their feasts.
A good man may punish me and rebuke me in
    kindness,
  but I will never accept honour from evil men,
because I am always praying against their evil
  deeds.   Psalm 141:1–5

Some of us may well feel the need for saying these
words at the end of a day. We start off in the morning
feeling clean and fresh, ready for what the day may
bring; we end up in the evening hours feeling bes-
mirched. We have not always guarded our tongue, so
that things have been said that are regretted afterwards.
The temptations that those in business or work situations may have to face can provide stress and tension;
they are often difficult to withstand. There are those
around us who are ready to laugh at our beliefs, and
thus sometimes, in groups of our peers, we can feel very
alone.

  And so it is, that in the evening hour we turn to the

One who has seen everything that has happened, understood us as we have not been able perhaps to understand ourselves, and who knows our heart now as we stand before him.

A part of the wonderful gift of our salvation is that forgiveness is continually available for us. Now, at the end of the day, we may bring him all that disturbs us about our behaviour and ask for that forgiveness. We can seek his help as we contemplate tomorrow; our weaknesses may be confided to him. This psalm begins with a plea with which we can easily associate ourselves. Our hope is in God, our whole being seeks both to praise him, and to intreat him, and we shall not be confounded.

May my desire for your forgiveness and my trust
in your salvation indeed be as an evening sacrifice.

Goodnight, Lord

52

Finally, build up your strength in union with the Lord and by means of his mighty power. Put on all the armour that God gives you, so that you will be able to stand up against the Devil's evil tricks. For we are not fighting against human beings but against the wicked spiritual forces in the heavenly world, the rulers, authorities, and cosmic powers of this dark age. So put on God's armour now! Then when the evil day comes, you will be able to resist the enemy's attacks; and after fighting to the end, you will still hold your ground.

Ephesians 6:10–13

This is a picture of the soldier of Christ that is often used, a wonderful flannelgraph talk for young people, as piece after piece of the armour is put on to the "body".

As we read and understand these words we realize the protection available to us as Christians against an enemy who, because he is God's enemy, is also ours. We have pledged ourselves to God and therefore must face that which is his opposite, evil.

If we fail to realize that there are "principalities and powers" then we will fail to recognize the "evil tricks", and our Christian life may be lived at a low ebb.

There are those who make a ceremony of putting on the armour day by day. This can be a snare, for when we rely literally on this act, if there should come a time when it is not done, we can feel vulnerable by believing that we are unprotected. Instead, we should perhaps make sure that by constant communication with God we are always ready for whatever may come; for our initial commitment to him meant that all this protection became ours. What we need to do is to undersatnd how to use this armour. The knowledge of our righteousness through Christ is as a breast plate, faith is indeed a shield, for believing in the One belittles belief in the enemy. Assurance of salvation and knowledge of the Scriptures, God's Word, makes us strong and powerful.

Paul, through these verses, is reminding us that it is God's power, and our realization of all that we have in him and through our redemption in Christ, that is our protection and our weapon against "wicked spiritual forces". We are therefore armoured and may thus stand our ground.

Thank you, Father, that I am armoured against the wiles of the evil one through Christ. Help me always to stand ready by my union with you.

Goodnight, Lord

53

I look to the mountains;
  where will my help come from?
My help will come from the LORD,
  who made heaven and earth.
He will not let you fall;
  your protector is always awake.
The protector of Israel
  never dozes or sleeps.
The LORD will guard you;
  he is by your side to protect you.
The sun will not hurt you during the day,
  nor the moon during the night.
The LORD will protect you from all danger;
  he will keep you safe.
He will protect you as you come and go
  now and for ever.

Psalm 121

The church which I attend has a large stained glass window at the east end. It is natural to look at it.

It is not so natural and easy to lift the eyes up higher, but the first time I did just that I found myself looking at a small rosette type of window. The centre is bright red, with small panes of blues and greens set around.

Having seen it once I forgot about it until by accident my eyes went up again, and once more I found myself looking at that red circlet. Now, every time I see it I feel

110

a sense of joy, as if I have found something precious. The extraordinary thing is that I always find it by accident; some Sundays I do not even see it because I don't look up high enough.

How often do we keep our eyes so fixed downwards that we miss out on all that is above? On the ordinary level we can miss so much – and there is a tremendous amount of mess and dirt close to the ground.

Our psalm speaks of mountains; mountains can be breathtakingly beautiful. But in the same sentence the psalmist asks where he will find help, knowing that the mountains of his country cannot give him the help that he needs. Our help does not come from nature or possessions, or from anything else in which we may be tempted to put our trust; it comes from the Lord.

The psalmist has the assurance that whenever he needs help he can find it in God. We need, however, to keep that assurance ever in mind. The Lord is our constant protector; he will never fail us.

We may be inclined to forget, just as I so often do and therefore miss the beauty of the church window. Yet it is always there to be seen. So, too, we can rest in the knowledge that our God will not fail us: "Now and forever" means always.

✻✻✻

Thank you, Father, for the reminder that you are my help and protector. Keep me leaning hard on this truth day by day.

Goodnight, Lord

Fount Paperbacks

Fount is one of the leading paperback publishers of religious books and below are some of its recent titles.

☐ THROUGH SEASONS OF THE HEART
John Powell   £4.95
☐ WORDS OF LIFE FROM JOHN THE BELOVED
Frances Hogan   £2.95
☐ MEISTER ECKHART Ursula Fleming   £2.95
☐ CHASING THE WILD GOOSE Ron Ferguson   £2.95
☐ A GOOD HARVEST Rita Snowden   £2.50
☐ UNFINISHED ENCOUNTER Bob Whyte   £5.95
☐ FIRST STEPS IN PRAYER Jean-Marie Lustiger   £2.95
☐ IF THIS IS TREASON Allan Boesak   £2.95
☐ RECLAIMING THE CHURCH Robin Greenwood   £2.95
☐ GOD WITHIN US John Wijngaards   £2.95
☐ GOD'S WORLD Trevor Huddleston   £2.95
☐ A CALL TO WITNESS Oliver McTernan   £2.95
☐ GOODNIGHT LORD Georgette Butcher   £2.95
☐ FOR GOD'S SAKE Donald Reeves   £3.50
☐ GROWING OLDER Una Kroll   £2.95
☐ THROUGH THE YEAR WITH FRANCIS OF ASSISI
Murray Bodo   £2.95

All Fount Paperbacks are available at your bookshop or newsagent, or they can be ordered by post from Fount Paperbacks, Cash Sales Department, G.P.O. Box 29, Douglas, Isle of Man. Please send purchase price plus 22p per book, maximum postage £3. Customers outside the UK send purchase price, plus 22p per book. Cheque, postal order or money order. No currency.

NAME (Block letters) _____

ADDRESS _____

_____

_____

While every effort is made to keep prices low, it is sometimes necessary to increase them at short notice. Fount Paperbacks reserve the right to show new retail prices on covers which may differ from those previously advertised in the text or elsewhere.